COCKTASTIC CHRISTMAS

First published 2017 V.02 by Retro Inc Books
www.retroinc.co.uk
© 2017

ISBN 978-1979360074

Ella Cotton

Cocktastic Cock wrapping paper

Christmas Stockings

Cock Christmas Tree

'Can you guess what your present is?'

Bunting

Colour and cut out bunting.

Christmas Tree Cock Angel

'Deck the halls with balls and willies,
Fa la la la la la la la!
'Tis the season to be jolly,
Fa la la la la la la la!'

A colour and cut out Cock Angel
for the top of your Christmas tree.

Sure to cause some 'Ho Ho Ho's' this
Holiday season!

Maybe add a halo of tinsel and sprinkle of glitter.

Christmas Cock Robin

Cock Socks

Christmas Cock Wreath

Noel Cock

Christmas Bauble

Mince Pies

Cock Candy Cane

Gingerbread Men

Pull my cracker

Chestnuts roasting on an open fire

Snow Cock

Alpine Ski Lodge

Willys Winter Wonderland

(Taken from Ella's forthcoming book)

Snowman

Frosty Knob the Snowman

Yule Cock Log

A special treat a Christmas

Who doesn't enjoy a tasty chocolate Yule
knob?

Yule Knob

Noël

Robin Mandala

An unusal 'Round Robin'

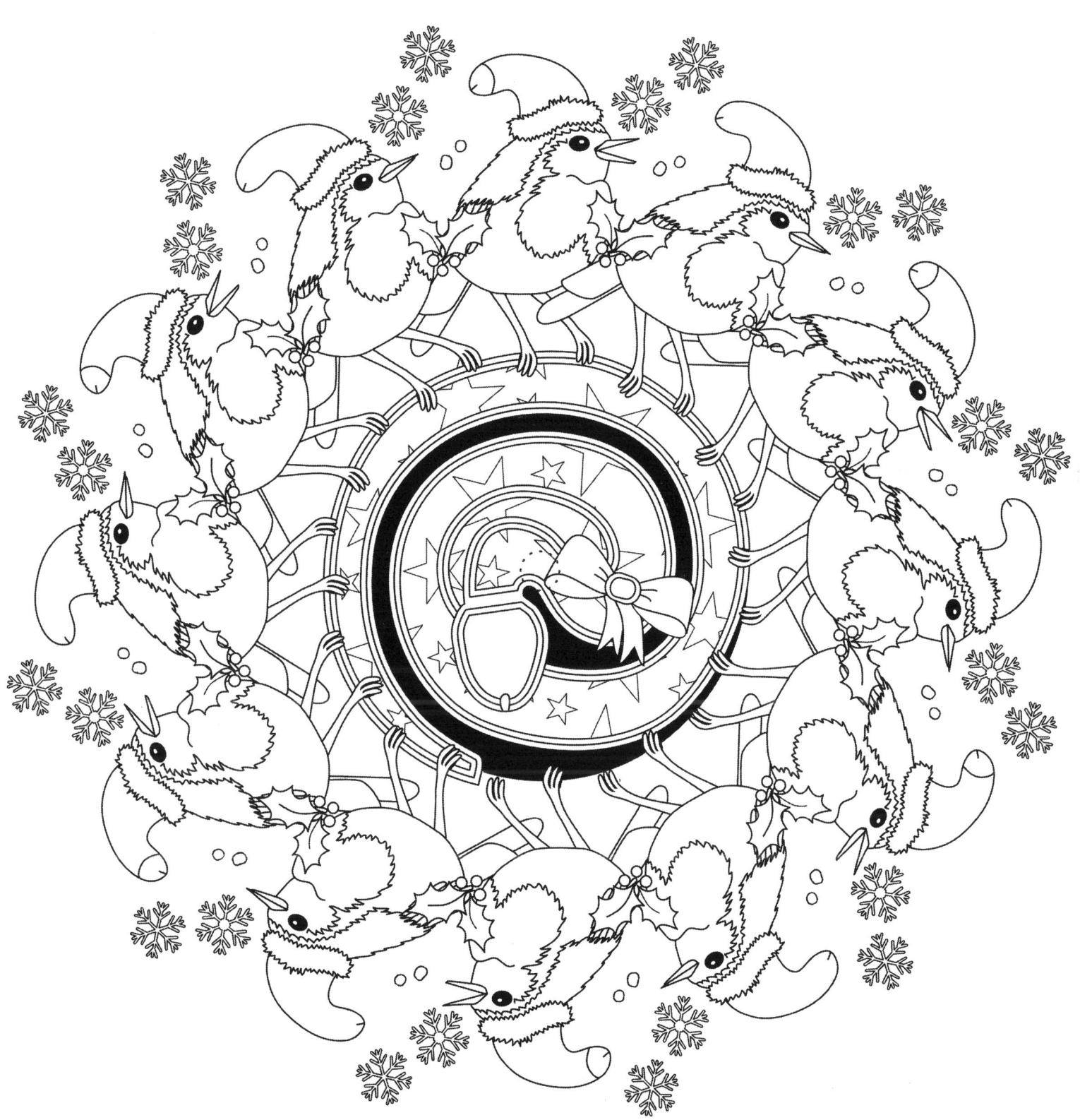

Bunting

More Colour and cut out bunting.

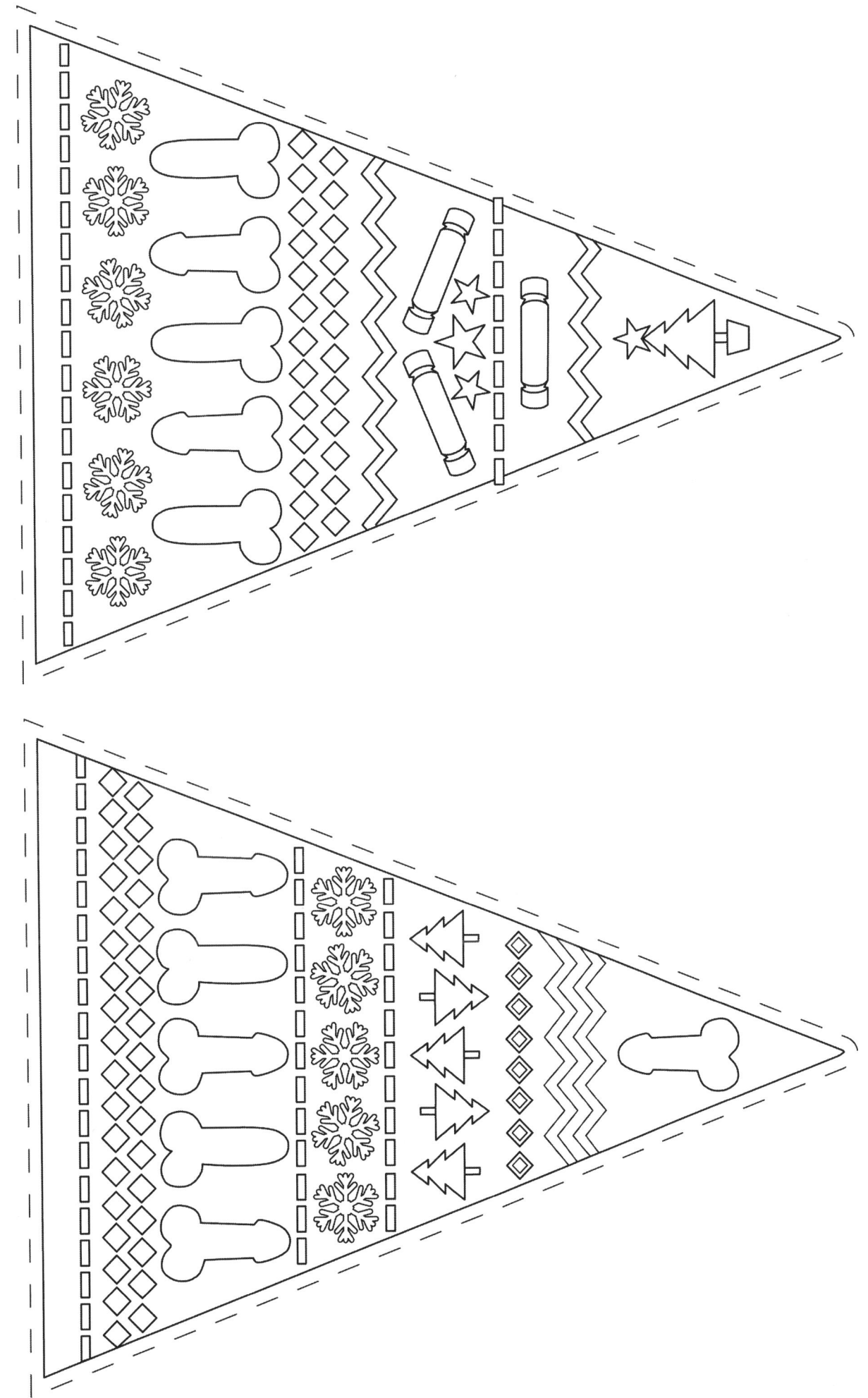

Holly Cock tree

Kiss under the mistletoe

Happy Holidays

Frosty Knob Snowman
Happy Holidays Card

HAPPY HOLIDAYS

Kaleidoscope

(of Christmas Cocks)

**Rude-olph the
Red Knobbed Reindeer**

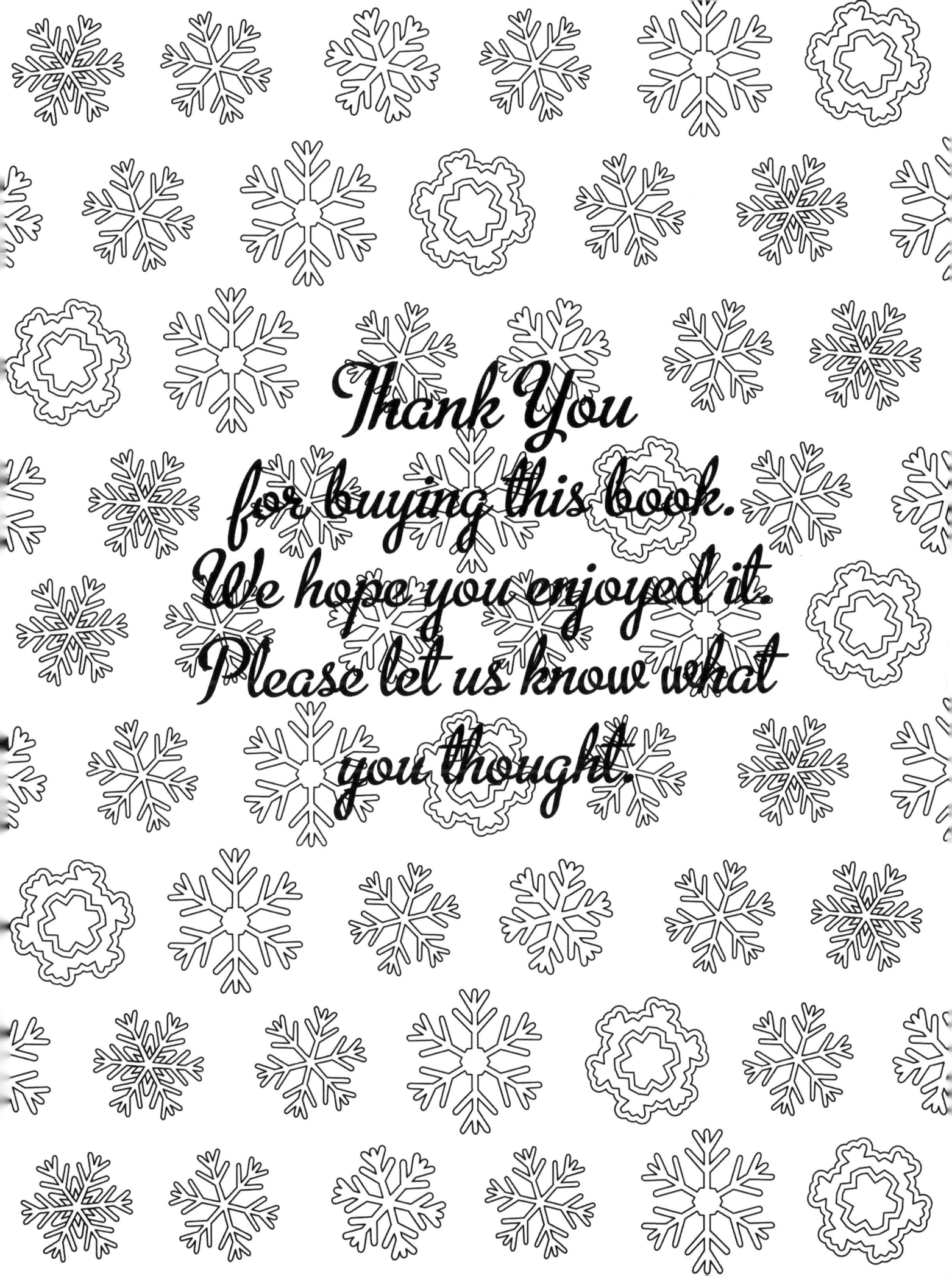

Gingerbread Men / Cocks

Ingredients
- 100g soft light brown sugar
- 100g golden syrup
- 230g plain flour
- Pinch of salt
- 1 heaped tsp bicarbonate of soda
- 2 tsp ground ginger
- Pinch of cinnamon
- 50g unsalted butter

Method
1. Preheat oven 190'C/Gas mark 5
2. Heat butter, sugar and syrup until dissolved then leave to cool.
3. Mix into the dry ingredients and make a dough.
4. Chill the dough in the fridge for about 30 minutes.
5. Roll out the dough to about 1/4 inch thick and cut into gingerbread men/cocks. Place on grease proofed trays allowing space to spread.
6. Cook for 10-15 minutes.
7. Cool on a wire rack and then decorate.

retroinc.co.uk

Thank you for purchasing this book.
We hope you enjoy it.

Please contact us with any comments you may have.
It's great to hear from readers.

Please check out Ella's other adult colouring books on Amazon:

Pussytastic - Colourful Lady Gardens ISBN 978-1545518533

Cocktastic! Colourful Cocks - Willies in Art ISBN 978-1539874683

Find out more via our website or facebook page:
facebook.com/retroincbooks

Twitter @retrobooks @ellacottonart
www.retroinc.co.uk

Printed in Great Britain
by Amazon